Pebble Plus

What Makes a Family?

Families Work Together

by Martha E. H. Rustad

PEBBLE
a capstone imprint

Pebble Plus is published by Pebble
1710 Roe Crest Drive,
North Mankato, Minnesota 56003
www.mycapstone.com

Library of Congress Cataloging-in-Publication Data
Library of Congress Cataloging-in-Publication Data is available on the Library of Congress website.
ISBN 978-1-9771-0904-0 (library binding)
ISBN 978-1-9771-1052-7 (paperback)
ISBN 978-1-9771-1274-3 (eBook PDF)

Editorial Credits
Marissa Kirkman, editor; Cynthia Della-Rovere, designer;
Eric Gohl, media researcher; Tori Abraham, production specialist

Image Credits
iStockphoto: Morsa Images, 11, SolStock, 21, Steve Debenport, 19; Shutterstock: Anutr Yossundara, 17, DGLimages, 7, Dragon
Images, 1, LightField Studios, cover, Lopolo, 9, Monkey Business Images, 5, Sergey Novikov, 15, wavebreakmedia, 13
Design Elements: Shutterstock

All internet sites appearing in back matter were available and accurate when this book was sent to press.

Note to Parents and Teachers
The What Makes a Family? set supports national standards related to social studies. This book describes and illustrates how
families work together. The images support early readers in understanding the text. The repetition of words and phrases helps
early readers learn new words. This book also introduces early readers to subject-specific vocabulary words, which are defined
in the Glossary section. Early readers may need assistance to read some words and to use the Table of Contents, Glossary, Read
More, Internet Sites, Critical Thinking Questions, and Index sections of the book.

Printed and bound in China.
001654

Table of Contents

Let's Work Together. 4

At Home 6

In the Community 14

Glossary 22

Read More 23

Internet Sites. 23

Critical Thinking Questions 24

Index 24

Let's Work Together

Families work together.

They help each other every day.

Family members support

each other. They keep their

homes and neighborhoods safe.

At Home

Camila's family works together at home. Camila helps her dad wash the dishes. Her brother picks up toys. Together they keep their home clean.

Aaron's family works outside together. His stepdad weeds the garden. Aaron and his sisters rake the leaves. They make their yard look nice.

Jojo's family works together on their farm. Her grandpa and brother feed the chickens. Jojo helps her aunt milk a cow. They sell eggs and milk for money.

Ali's mom helps him with his homework. She helps him understand what to do. She helps to make it fun.

In the Community

Families work together in the community. Oliver's family volunteers at the library. They shelve books and read to kids.

Finn's family helps neighbors.
His older sister babysits the
neighbors' kids. Finn gets mail
for Mr. Smith. He walks
Mr. Smith's dog too.

Nadia's family works at a soup kitchen. Her parents cut vegetables. Her brother washes dishes. Together they help feed people in need.

Families work together at home.

They take care of each other.

Families help in the community.

They work together to make

the world better.

Glossary

aunt—the sister of a person's mother or father; an aunt also can be the wife of a person's uncle

community—a group of people who live in the same town or area

farm—a place where people grow crops and raise animals

grandpa—the father of a person's mother or father

library—a place with books, magazines, and videos for you to borrow

neighbor—a person who lives in a home next to yours or in the same area as your home

neighborhood—a particular area of a town or city, especially near your home

soup kitchen—a place that feeds meals to hungry or homeless people in need

stepdad—a man who marries someone's parent after the death or divorce of the person's father

volunteer—to offer to do something without getting paid

Read More

James, Emily. *How To Be a Good Citizen: A Question and Answer Book About Citizenship*. Character Matters. North Mankato, MN: Capstone Press, 2015.

Pemberton, Rose. *Why Do We Have to Do Chores?* The Common Good. New York: PowerKids Press, 2018.

Zietlow Miller, Pat. *Be Kind*. New York: Roaring Book Press, 2018.

Internet Sites

Backyard Chicken Chores for Kids
https://www.lifeinminnesota.com/backyard-chicken-chores-for-kids/

Can-Do Kids' Chores
https://www.scholastic.com/parents/family-life/social-emotional-learning/social-skills-for-kids/can-do-kids-chores.html

Volunteer at Your Library
http://safeyoutube.net/w/MGVe

Critical Thinking Questions

1. How do you help your family with work?

2. What jobs do you do at home?

3. How can you help your community?

Index

cleaning up, 6, 18
farms, 10
helping in the community, 14, 16, 18, 20
helping neighbors, 16
homes, 4, 6, 20
homework, 12

neighborhoods, 4
stepdads, 8
taking care of animals, 10, 18
volunteering, 14, 18
washing dishes, 6, 16
working outside, 8, 10
yards, 8